1 MONTH OF FREE READING

at

www.ForgottenBooks.com

By purchasing this book you are eligible for one month membership to ForgottenBooks.com, giving you unlimited access to our entire collection of over 1,000,000 titles via our web site and mobile apps.

To claim your free month visit:

www.forgottenbooks.com/free1116854

* Offer is valid for 45 days from date of purchase. Terms and conditions apply.

ISBN 978-0-331-39095-7
PIBN 11116854

This book is a reproduction of an important historical work. Forgotten Books uses state-of-the-art technology to digitally reconstruct the work, preserving the original format whilst repairing imperfections present in the aged copy. In rare cases, an imperfection in the original, such as a blemish or missing page, may be replicated in our edition. We do, however, repair the vast majority of imperfections successfully; any imperfections that remain are intentionally left to preserve the state of such historical works.

Forgotten Books is a registered trademark of FB &c Ltd.
Copyright © 2018 FB &c Ltd.
FB &c Ltd, Dalton House, 60 Windsor Avenue, London, SW19 2RR.
Company number 08720141. Registered in England and Wales.

For support please visit www.forgottenbooks.com

STATE OF NEW HAMPSHIRE
STATE TAX COMMISSION

UNIFORM MUNICIPAL ACCOUNTS

Financial Report

OF THE

Town of Stark, N. H.

IN COOS COUNTY
FOR THE FISCAL YEAR ENDING
JANUARY 31

1932

CERTIFICATE

This is to certify that the information contained in this report was taken from the official records and is complete to the best of our knowledge and belief.

J. E. MONTGOMERY,
E. A. SCOTT, } Selectmen.
ALBERT R. EMERY,

URANIA H. CROTEAU, Treasurer.

Selectmen's Report

Valuation

Resident real estate	$176,524.00
Non-resident real estate	281,186.00
Whole number horses, 85	6,448.00
Whole number cows, 195	10,772.00
Whole number neat stock, 34	1,336.00
Whole number sheep, 11	88.00
Whole number mules, 1	50.00
Whole number fowls, 90	90.00
Value of boats and launches	300.00
Value of wood and lumber	2,354.00
Value of gasoline pumps	1,200.00
Value of stock in trade	1,000.00
Value of mills and machinery	3,900.00
Total valuation	$489,008.00
Whole number polls, 192	384.00

Assessments

State tax	$ 1,134.00
County tax	1,888.47
Highway money per statute	1,222.52
Highway money per vote	3,000.00
State aid construction	762.00
State aid maintenance	1,525.00
State aid Mill Brook bridge	1,500.00
Legislative special	1,000.00
Current expenses	500.00
School money per statute and vote	4,800.00
Total assessments	$ 17,331.99
Less revenue and credit	2,300.00
	$ 15,031.99
Less 192 polls @ $2.00	384.00
	$ 14,647.99

TOWN OF STARK, N. H.

Adding in assessing 16.25

Property tax ....$ 14,664.24
                                                                    384.00

Total ....$ 15,048.24
Rate of taxation, $3.00 per $100. Poll tax $2.00

CERTIFICATE

This is to certify that the information contained in this report was taken from official records and is complete to the best of our knowledge and belief.

Date, January 30, 1932.

J. E. MONTGOMERY,
E. A. SCOTT,
ALBERT EMERY,
Selectmen.
URANIA H. CROTEAU,
Treasurer.

TOWN OF STARK, N. H.

Balance

Assets

Cash in hands of treasurer...$		763.00
ACCOUNTS DUE TO THE TOWN:		
Due from State:		
Bounties		14.80
Due from County:		
(a) 1928 account ....$	96.57	
(b) 1930 account	118.48	
(c) 1931 account	62.00	
	$	277.05
Other bills due Town:		
(a) Taxes bought by Town..........$1,815.23		
	$	1,815.23
Taxes not collected:		
(a) Levy of 1927, H. W. Stone $	358.36	
(b) Levy of 1929, M. A. Osgood	12.00	
(c) Levy of 1930, M. A. Osgood	15.30	
(d) Levy of 1931, M. A. Osgood	277.88	
	$	663.54
Total assets ....$		3,533.62
Excess of liabilities over assets...................$		7,906.21
Grand total ....$		11,439.83
Net Debt—January 31, 1931...............................		4,598.26
Net Debt—January 31, 1932...............................		7,906.21
Increase of debt		3,307.95

Sheet

Liabilities

ACCOUNTS OWED BY THE TOWN:
Due to School Districts:
  (a) Dog licenses ....$ 139.83
  (b) Balance of appropriation........ 2,300.00

                                          $ 2,439.83
Outstanding Temporary Loans in Anticipation of Taxes.......................... $ 9,000.00

Total liabilities .... $ 11,439.83

Grand Total ....$ 11,439.83

Receipts

Receipts

Current Revenue:
From Local Taxes:

Property taxes committed to collector, 1931	$15,054.24	
Less discount and abatement, 1931	100.00	
Less uncollected, 1931	944.08	
Property taxes current year, actually collected	13,875.56	
Poll taxes, current year, actually collected 124 @ $2.00	248.00	
Property and poll taxes, previous years actually collected	151.66	
Total of above collections		$ 14,275.22
Tax sales redeemed		225.14

From State:

For Highways and Bridges:		
(a) For State Aid maintenance	$ 8,142.97	
(b) For State Aid construction	1,391.55	
(c) For Trunk Line maintenance S. A. construction, special	1,456.69	
(d) For Trunk Line construction Mill Brook bridge	748.56	
Interest and dividend tax	598.73	
Abatement tax	283.09	
Railroad tax	2,651.78	
Savings bank tax	263.20	
Savings bank tax	114.08	
Fighting forest fires	12.96	
Bounties	23.60	
		$ 15,687.21

From Local Sources, Except Taxes:

Dog taxes	$ 71.23
Sale of cement	1.53
Received Mill Brook bridge	4.62
Rent of town property	76.00
Received from C. N. R. R.	85.20
Standard Oil Co., refund check	16.50
Town of Dummer, plowing roads	100.00
Cemetery lot	10.00
J. E. Montgomery, foreman	66.22
Registration of motor vehicles,	

TOWN OF STARK, N. H.

Payments

Payments

Current Maintenance Expenses:
General Government:
Town officers' salaries .... $	848.75
Town officers' expenses	212.18
Expenses town hall and other town buildings	36.51

Protection of Persons and Property:
Police department, including care of tramps	14.00
Fire department, including forest fires	112.90
Insurance	48.00
Bounties	14.80

Health:
Health department, including hospitals	5.00
Vital statistics	5.25

Highways and Bridges:
State Aid maintenance	9,751.72
Town maintenance	5,840.08
General expenses of highway dept., including watering troughs ...	276.45

Charities:
Town poor	1,253.65
County poor	62.00

Patriotic Purposes:
Aid to soldiers and their families	76.00

Public Service Enterprises:
Cemeteries, including hearse hire ...	117.78

Unclassified:
Running Town lines	60.50
Refund check	2.54

——————$ 18,738.11

Interest:
Paid on temporary loans in anticipation of taxes	$ 972.50

Outlay for New Construction and Permanent Improvements:
Highways and Bridges—State Aid construction	$ 2,126.42
Highways and Bridges—S. A. bridge	$ 2,707.45

Receipts

1931 permits	244.25		
Registration of motor vehicles, 1932 permits	152.59		
		$	828.14

Receipts Other Than Current Revenue:
Temporary loans in anticipation of taxes during year $18,000.00

Total receipts other than current revenue .... $ 18,000.00

Total receipts from all sources.... $ 49,015.71
Cash on hand February 1, 1931.... 549.98

Grand Total .... $ 49,565.69

Payments

Federal Aid Construction, S. A. special		$ 2,535.74

Indebtedness:

Payments on temporary loans in anticipation of taxes		$ 14,000.00

Payments to Other Governmental Divisions:

Taxes paid to State	$1,134.00	
Taxes paid to County	1,888.47	
Payments to School Districts	4,700.00	
Total payments to other governmental divisions		$ 48,802.69
Cash on hand Jan. 31, 1932		763.00
Grand Total		$ 49,565.69

Schedule of Town Property

Description	Value
Town Hall, land and buildings................$	850.00
Furniture and equipment	200.00
Libraries, lands and buildings................	800.00
Police Department, land and buildings.....	15.00
Fire Department, land and buildings........	75.00
Highway Department, equipment	4,300.00
Schools, lands and buildings..................	4,500.00
Total .... $	10,740.00

Detail Statement of Assets

Cash in hands of treasurer................................ $		763.00
Due from State, bounties		14.80
Due from County		277.05
Taxes not collected:		
Levy of 1927................................	$358.36	
Levy of 1929................................	12.00	
Levy of 1930................................	15.30	
Levy of 1931................................	277.88	
Total taxes not collected...............		663.54
Taxes bought by Town:		
Riley S. Lunn, bal. of tax, 1923............ $	56.48	
Fred McFarland, tax, 1923	12.34	
Emma L. Abbott, bal. tax, 1924............	20.35	
Riley S. Lunn, tax, 1924......................	98.32	
Emma L. Abbott, tax, 1925..................	23.38	
Emma L. Abbott, tax, 1926	21.12	
Samuel F. Goodwin, tax, 1926.............	2.66	
Riley S. Lunn, tax, 1926......................	91.00	

TOWN OF STARK, N. H.

John Ramsey Estate, bal. tax, 1926	1.67
Riley Lunn, tax, 1927	98.07
John Ramsey Estate, tax, 1927	5.83
Samuel F. Goodwin Estate, tax, 1927	2.64
Emma L. Abbott, tax, 1927	23.10
Robert Emerson, tax, 1930	12.25
Martha Emerson, bal. tax, 1930	46.13
Samuel F. Goodwin Estate, tax, 1930	4.35
Francis Aubit, tax, 1931	9.75
Emma L. Abbott, tax, 1931	31.95
Eugene Bassett, tax, 1931	30.17
Chas. Ducharme, tax, 1931	33.05
R. J. Emerson, tax, 1931	30.65
Martha Emerson, tax, 1931	50.25
Gertrude Emery, tax, 1931	15.75
Elmer Forbush, tax, 1931	18.75
Tom Forbush, tax, 1931	17.75
Samuel Goodwin, tax, 1931	4.75
Orange Holbrook, tax, 1931	26.75
Delivan Howland, tax, 1931	5.25
Ollie Jackson, tax, 1931	99.29
Valida Keezer, tax, 1931	8.25
Perley Lee, tax, 1931	13.75
Henry Lee, tax, 1931	10.75
Riley S. Lunn, tax, 1931	105.35
Chas. and Aaron Potter, tax, 1931	62.93
John Ramsey Estate, tax, 1931	9.25
Geo. A. Veazie, tax, 1931	13.75
Cushing & Frizzel, tax, 1931	10.75
Luther Baldwin, tax, 1931	2.25
Lewis Mayhew, tax, 1931	4.75
Larkin Astle and Turgeron, tax, 1931	5.53
Edgar Bacon, tax, 1928	2.63
Emma L. Abbott, tax, 1928	23.11
Samuel F. Goodwin, tax, 1928	2.63
Riley Lunn, tax, 1928	98.87
John Ramsey Estate, tax, 1928	5.84
Cold Stream Club, tax, 1928	2.63
Lewis Mayhew, tax, 1928	2.38
Elmer Forbush, tax, 1929	16.50
Samuel Goodwin, tax, 1929	4.50
Fred Hands, bal. tax, 1929	77.82
Harrison Keezer, bal. tax, 1929	21.50
Riley Lunn, tax, 1929	108.42

John Ramsey Estate, tax, 1929	9.00
Emma L. Abbott, tax, 1930	30.44
Elmer Forbush, tax, 1930	15.00
Harrison Keezer, bal tax, 1930	11.80
Riley S. Lunn, tax, 1930	96.65
Chas. and Aaron Potter, tax, 1930	57.20
John Ramsey Estate, tax, 1930	8.50
Geo. A. Veazie, tax, 1930	38.90
Town of Northumberland, tax, 1930	28.00
Cold Stream Club, tax, 1930	4.60
Mayhew P. Montgomery, tax, 1930	7.20
Total taxes bought by town	$ 1,815.23
Total assets	$ 3,533.62

Detail Statement of Payments

Detail 1. Town officers' salaries:
Current Maintenance Expenses
J. E. Montgomery, selectman...........$	125.00
E. A. Scott, selectman	125.00
Albert Emery, selectman	100.00
M. A. Osgood, collector, 1929........	.45
M. A. Osgood, collector, 1930........	2.58
M. A. Osgood, collector, 1931........	282.47
Urania Croteau, treasurer.............	50.00
Stella Lunn, town clerk	75.00
Una M. Cole, supervisor..............	8.00
Wilfred Oakes, supervisor	8.00
Urania Croteau, supervisor	8.00
R. J. Emerson, dog constable........	15.00
Henry Pike, auditor	5.00
C. A. Cole, moderator	4.00

$ 808.50

Detail 2. Town officers' expenses:
Edson C. Eastman, tax books, warrants$	10.16
Smith & Town, printing reports........	71.40
J. E. Montgomery, two trips to Berlin	8.00
Albert Emery, attending tax meeting...	4.00
E. A. Scott, attending tax meeting....	4.00
Automotive Service Bureau	4.73
E. A. Scott, car taking inventory.....	15.00
Groveton Advertiser, printing notice...	1.50
A. W. Rowell, dues assessors' meeting	2.00
Albert Emery, fire meeting expenses....	4.00
E. A. Scott, car hire.................	10.00
The Cooper Press, letter heads........	4.50
Edson C. Eastman, order book.........	12.25
Edmund Sullivan, attorney fees.......	10.50
Stella Lunn, issuing auto permits.....	27.75
Stella Lunn, copying checklist........	1.00
Stella Lunn, recording vital statistics	1.50
Urania Croteau, postage	2.00
Edson C. Eastman, supplies...........	2.69

14 TOWN OF STARK, N. H.

M. A. Osgood, telephone calls	1.20	
J. E. Montgomery, postage	5.00	
E. A. Scott, team hire, telephone	9.00	
M. A. Osgood, recording land sold	40.25	
		$ 252.43

Detail 3. Town Hall expenses:

B. F. Cummings, repairs to piano $	5.50	
Sim Veazie, repairing platform	4.38	
Reed Dixon, brooms	6.00	
Sim Veazie, lumber	1.50	
Wilfred Oakes, janitor, cleaning	14.50	
Urania Croteau, supplies	4.63	
	$	36.51

Detail 4. Police Department:

Lewis O. Pike $	4.00	
Harry C. Howe	10.00	
	$	14.00

Detail 5. Insurance:

George M. Stevens, tractor $	23.00	
George M. Stevens, Town Hall	25.00	
	$	48.00

Detail 6. Fire Department:

Harper Corkum, fighting fire $	.80
Herman McGuire, fighting fire	.80
George McGuire, fighting fire	.80
Aram Abbott, fighting fire	7.20
Len Peabody, fighting fire	.80
Myron Cole, fighting fire	.80
Jot Lary, fighting fire	.80
Frank Burgess, fighting fire	.80
Vernon Bickford, fighting fire	.80
Irving Cole, fighting fire	.80
Cad Peabody, fighting fire	.80
Leon Ray, fighting fire	.80
Alex Silver, fighting fire	.80
Allie Forbush, fighting fire	.80
Joe Cote, fighting fire	.80
Ernest Perron, fighting fire	2.40
Ollie Jackson, fighting fire	.80
Herbert Hart, fighting fire	.80
Edgar Bacon, fighting fire	.80

TOWN OF STARK, N. H.

Chas. Dorr, fighting fire	.80
Fred Hunter, fighting fire	.80
R. C. Montgomery, fighting fire	2.40
John Pepaw, fighting fire	7.20
S. B. Abbott, fighting fire	7.20
Harold Faulkingham, fighting fire	.80
Albert Emery, deputy, fighting fire	3.00
Albert Lapointe, fighting fire	1.60
Harold Montgomery, fighting fire	1.60
Roy Cole, fighting fire	1.60
Benny House, fighting fire	1.60
Wilfred Oakes, fighting fire	1.60
Howard Conley, fighting fire	1.60
James Lunn, fighting fire	1.60
Bradley Lunn, fighting fire	1.60
Elmer McFarland, fighting fire	1.60
Phillip Croteau, fighting fire	1.60
Glenn Lunn, fighting fire	1.60
Earle Pearson, fighting fire	1.60
Sam Oakes, fighting fire	1.60
Allie Sessions, fighting fire	1.60
John Croteau, fighting fire	1.60
Riley Lunn, fighting fire	1.60
Gilbert Rogers, fighting fire	1.60
Clifton Abbott, fighting fire	1.60
R. C. Montgomery, trucks	4.00
Phillip Croteau, car	2.00
Riley Lunn, car	2.00
J. E. Montgomery, warden	3.00

$ 85.20

Albert Emery, trip to Berlin $	4.00
Albert Emery, expenses	1.95
J. W. Emery, trip to Berlin	4.00
J. W. Emery, expenses	5.75

$ 15.70

J. E. Montgomery, posting notice $	4.00
Neil McKinnon, posting notice	4.00
Albert Emery, posting notice	4.00

$ 12.00

$ 112.90

Charities

Detail 8. County poor:
Wilfred Oakes, feeding tramps............ $ 62.50

Public Service Enterprise

Detail 9. Cemeteries:
State Highway Department, paint........$	15.03	
Sim Veazie, painting cemetery fence....	38.50	
George Hill, mowing and cleaning........	54.25	
R. J. Emerson, mowing	10.00	
		$ 117.78

Health and Sanitation

Detail 10. Health Department:
William Emery, service	$	5.00
Stella Lunn, recording vital statistics	$	5.25

Town Poor Account

Detail 7. Charities:
Sada Miles Case:
Albert Johnson, care ....$	84.00	
Exilda Hill, board and care	459.50	
Dr. Brown, medical attendance	16.00	
		$ 559.50

Nina Smith Case:
R. C. Montgomery, milk ....$	2.40	
Urania Croteau, supplies	.75	
Paul Cole, supplies	14.34	
Bars Emery, supplies	1.04	
Atlantic Tea Company	7.02	
R. H. Johnson, attendance	2.00	
Nina Smith, cash paid	203.00	
		$ 230.55

Jennie Roberts Case:
Lydia Gillanders, care ....$	276.50	
Clifton Albert, repairing house............	7.00	
Hugh Cole, windows and banking........	7.00	
C. A. Cole, wood	36.00	
Leon Kay, splitting wood......................	11.00	
S. B. Abbott, supplies	2.10	
		$ 330.60

A. J. Martin Case:
George Hill, digging grave ....$ 7.00

J. H. Finley, burial................................ 99.50
Rev. George Thomas 2.00

$ 108.50

William Hopkins Case:
St. Louis Hospital .... $ 24.50

$1,253.65

Unemployment Fund
Detail 11. State Aid Maintenance:
Riley Lunn ....$ 35.00
Walter Perkins 45.50
Ollie Jackson 43.75
Tom Forbush 43.75
Alex Silver 43.75
John Pepaw 7.00
Albert Lapointe 43.75
Phillip Croteau 14.00
Sim Veazie 45.50
S. B. Abbott 43.75
Riley Lunn, cedar posts.................. 35.00
J. E. Montgomery, cedar posts....... 11.55
                                                       87.50

$ 499.80

State Aid Maintenance
Sam Oakes ....$ 22.75
R. C. Montgomery 1,152.49
Eddie Hamel 124.24
Leon Kay 124.89
Bars Emery 23.14
Dorance Gilcris 90.22
Arthur Hamel 21.58
Bert Emery 15.75
Ed Tilton 15.75
Norman Hickey 10.50
Phillip Croteau 36.00
J. E. Montgomery 861.32
John Pepaw 26.83
Glenn Lunn 44.25
Dan Cowan 136.89
J. A. Scott & Son............................ 111.00
Myron Cole 533.00
Jot Lary 24.50
Albert Emery 475.23

E. A. Scott	7.00
Amos Emery	21.00
Urania Croteau	36.00
Sim Veazie	91.00
Vernon Bickford	450.69
Alex Silver	135.33
Len Peabody	106.75
Andrew Leighton	229.33
Archie Schoff	107.14
Ovila Fountain	3.50
Judson Delong	80.00
Hugh Cole	21.00
Albert Lapointe	75.84
Gilbert Hickey	11.08
James Croteau	44.33
Tom Forbush	101.30
Bert Lyman	39.08
Wilfred Oakes	191.33
Sam Pearson	85.75
Clifton Abbott	196.00
Walter Perkins	135.72
Aram Abbott	93.14
James Lunn	21.00
Harold Faulkingham	212.14
Albion Leighton	157.00
Herman Maguire	203.39
Ollie Jackson	119.00
Orange Holbrook	63.00
Gideon Hamel, posts	44.45
Frank Hall	153.80
S. B. Abbott	140.00
Allie Sessions	65.14
George Hill	192.89
William Hand	208.64
Eugene Bassett	10.50
Elbert Scott	91.39
Herbert Miles	5.25
Harold Pearson	102.00
Riley Lunn	284.83
Glenn Miles	55.61
Curtis Hardware Company	1.35
Paul Cole	196.67
Will Hopkins	59.50
Carol Gilcris	286.44
Ethel Miles	40.45

TOWN OF STARK, N. H.

John Croteau	137.42
Chas. A. Cole, gravel	117.20
Chas. A. Cole, posts	10.50
F. E. Moses, sand	48.40
Bars Emery, posts	6.30
J. E. Montgomery, mileage	38.80
J. E. Montgomery, check to town	66.22

$9,251.92

Tractor Account
Detail 12. Town Maintenance:

Standard Oil Company, gas $	47.50
Maine Steel Products Co., repairs	33.00
Howland's Garage, gas and supplies	24.78
C. D. Gilcris, labor on plow, gas	102.28
Ernest Kiser, operating	159.00
Albert Emery & Son, gas	9.61
J. A. Scott & Son, gas	4.40
Gilbert Hickey, labor	7.75
Urania Croteau, gas	5.70
Walter Perkins, labor on plow	125.50
Northern Road Equipment Co., sprockett	75.00
Amos Emery, moving tractor	8.00
R. J. Emerson, labor	15.00
E. A. Scott, team	13.25
Harry Bilodeau, repairing	17.10
Northern Road Equipment Co., repairs	45.75
Groveton Paper Co., repairs	52.12
M. A. Osgood, oil	32.20
Colonial Garage, repairs	18.47
Stark Spring Water Co., gas	9.69
William Lenhert, gas	1.90
Central Garage, battery	7.50
Ernest Kiser, labor, repairs	12.75

$ 828.25

Shoveling Snow

R. J. Emerson, labor $	10.00
Paul St. Francis	7.00
Phillip Croteau	7.00
Riley S. Lunn	28.00
Norman Hickey	7.00
Bert Emery	21.00
Gilbert Hickey	7.00
Wilfrid Oakes	18.50

TOWN OF STARK, N. H.

Albert Lapointe	17.50
Frank Gibson	10.50
George Hill	10.50
A. A. Abbott	10.50
S. B. Abbott	11.67
John Pepaw	11.67
Harold Montgomery	3.50
J. E. Montgomery	20.47
Amos Emery	7.00
Harold Pearson	17.50
Samuel Oakes	10.50
Charles Ducharme	5.25
Elmer McFarland	6.42
Samuel Pearson	7.98
Charles Potter	8.75
William Emery	10.50
Allie Sessions	13.50
Walter Perkins	9.50
Eddie Hamel	1.75
Sim Veazie	3.50
Bars Emery	7.00
Glenn Miles	3.50
Herbert Miles	3.50
Albert Emery	3.50
Harry Stone	5.25
Paul R. Cole, team	8.17
Bert Lyman	3.50
Wilfred Oakes	4.00
	$ 342.38

Truck, Plow

E. J. Graham, freight $	5.38
Standard Oil Company, gas	18.40
J. E. Montgomery, labor	18.09
Una M. Cole, gas	1.80
Albert Emery, labor	34.05
R. C. Montgomery	127.90
	$ 205.62

Paris Mfg. Company, lumber $	28.00
Hazen Cole, sharpening picks	8.25
Frank Smith Company, dynamite	26.00
Paul St. Francis, labor Nash Stream bridge	7.00
Brown Co., plank, Nash Stream bridge	165.15

TOWN OF STARK, N. H.

Groveton Paper Company, supplies	20.31
E. A. Scott, labor	7.00
R. J. Emerson, labor	19.00
John Ducharme, labor	1.75
J. B. Ingram, signs	24.41
R. J. Emerson, tarring bridge	12.00
Frank Gibson, tarring bridge	3.50
E. A. Scott, labor	10.00
Ralph Seavey, lumber, cement, rock	100.00
Amos Emery, hauling plank	14.00
Groveton Heating & Plumbing Co., supplies	54.16
Morris Israel, rubber boots	13.50
Highway Garage, paint	33.71
E. A. Scott, setting snow fence	3.50
P. I. Perkins, 200 ft. snow fence	29.00
F. E. Moses, 265 yds. sand	26.50
R. C. Montgomery, hauling gravel	44.74
C. D. Gilcris, repairs Leighton bridge	5.85
C. D. Gilcris, hauling gravel	42.00
Harold Pearson, labor	13.01
Walter Perkins, labor	13.01
Ernest Kiser, labor	13.01
Bert Emery, labor	10.50
J. E. Montgomery, labor	18.00
R. J. Emerson, labor ice jam	3.50
L. P. Abbott, sawing lumber	10.00
Orange Holbrook, gravel	6.20
Brown Company, gravel	7.60
Samuel Oakes, storing lumber	10.00
J. E. Montgomery, gas, oil for mixer	2.14
E. A. Scott, labor, ice jam	3.50
R. C. Montgomery, sanding	7.98
Albert Emery, sanding	2.40
	$ 820.18
R. J. Emerson, road agent	1,834.35
Ernest Kiser, road agent	1,809.30
	$4,463.83

Detail 13. General Expense of Highway Dept.:

Eldon Peabody	$ 24.85
F. L. Blake, road machine blade	8.00
F. L. Blake, road machine repairs	10.96
Austin Road Machine Co., repairs	16.05

Austin Road Machine Co., truck plow 180.00
Chas. Tillortison, supplies 27.60
Ollie Jackson, use of water tub, 1930-31 6.00
Bessie Hickey, use of water tub, 1931.... 3.00

$ 276.45

Unclassified

Detail 14. Bounties:
(a) Hedgehogs:

Edward Wintra .... $	1.00
Roy Cole	.40
John Pepaw	.60
Norman Lapointe	.20
Junior Hodgkins	.20
Charles West	2.00
Leonard Pearson	.60
Thomas Montgomery	.40
Phillip Oakes	.40
Bradley Lunn	.40
Norman Hickey	.40
Nate Foster	.20
Homer Emery	.20
Warren Sessions	.40
George Croteau	.40
Cecil Cote	.40
S. B. Abbott	.20
J. W. Emery	.80
M. A. Osgood	1.80
William Hands	.20
Roy Usher	.40
E. A. Scott	.40
Archie Schoff	.20
Albert Emery	.60
Dean Miles	.20
Alva Emery	.20
Winston Emery	.20
Leon Kay	1.40

$ 14.80

(b) Running Town Lines:
Howard T. Woodward .... $ 55.50
Gideon Hamel, moving horse 2.00

Gilbert Hickey, burying horse 3.00

$ 60.50

(c) Refunds:
Paul R. Cole, refund on auto tax .... $ 2.54
Detail 15. Patriotic Purposes:
Aid to soldiers and families .... $ 76.00
Detail 16. Mill Brook Bridge Account:
A. G. Roab, labor	$ 337.50
F. J. Bennett, labor	247.50
Robert Emerson	90.29
Samuel Oakes	91.29
Dorance Gilcris	50.18
Carol Gilcris	55.98
Wilfred Oakes	21.40
R. C. Montgomery	34.50
Albert Lapointe	14.00
S. B. Abbott	5.25
Arthur Hamel	7.00
Clifton Abbott	14.62
Sim Veazie	56.40
John Croteau	40.78
Samuel Pearson	37.15
J. A. Scott, team	33.84
Albert Emery, team	7.00
Riley Lunn	27.33
Tom Forbush	5.25
Phillip Croteau	5.25
James Croteau	1.75
Bert Lyman, labor	1.75
Len Peabody, labor	1.75
Ollie Jackson, labor	1.75
Ernest Kiser, labor	164.49
Ernest Kiser, lumber	39.90
Ernest Kiser, bags, nails, etc	20.88
Ira Noyes	50.00
Paul Cole	9.33
Myron Cole	1.75
Harold Pearson	6.00
Ralph Seavey, foreman	440.00
Ralph Seavey, telephone calls	2.40
Ralph Seavey, mileage	82.88
Canadian National R. R., freight	110.93
McGraw-McKelvey Co., lumber	48.80
Brown Company, lumber	139.58

City of Berlin, crushed rock	152.00
Selectmen of Stark, ship spikes	4.62
Urania Croteau, gasoline	15.07
Groveton Paper Company, lumber	57.83
H. A. Moore, files	.90
Hamlin Bros., cement	218.28
Sullivan Garage	44.88
Groveton Heating & Plumbing Co., supplies	7.42
	$2,807.45
Less credit for lumber, crushed rock and cement	100.00
	$2,707.45

Detail 17. Stark Leg. Special:

Samuel Oakes	$ 3.50
R. C. Montgomery	14.75
J. A Scott & Son	192.50
Vernon Bickford	91.00
Alex Silver	96.25
Len Peabody	99.75
Walter Perkins	103.25
J. E. Montgomery	177.00
Samuel Pearson	89.25
James Croteau	50.75
Wilfred Oakes	43.75
Tom Forbush	98.00
Ethel Miles	150.50
Bars Emery	61.25
Arthur Hamel	68.25
Phillip Croteau	52.50
Norman Hickey	21.00
Eddie Hamel	26.25
Riley Lunn	164.50
Glenn Lunn	21.00
Albert Lapointe	87.50
Ollie Jackson	103.25
Albert Emery	206.50
Sim Veazie	47.25
S. B. Abbott	89.25
Eugene Bassett	17.50
Canadian National R. R., freight	10.70
Paul Cole, land damage	125.00

TOWN OF STARK, N. H. 25

Bessie Hickey, land damage 123.79

$2,535.24

Detail 18. State Aid Construction:
John Pepaw ....$	53.67
Dan Cowan	66.50
J. A. Scott & Son	130.67
S. B. Abbott	42.00
George Hill	35.00
Eugene Bassett	21.00
Albert Emery	84.00
Myron Cole	141.33
Orange Holbrook	42.00
Ollie Jackson	59.50
Albert Lapointe	55.42
Gilbert Hickey	55.42
Harold Pearson	120.00
Riley Lunn	70.53
Bars Emery	42.00
Arthur Hamel	44.92
Dorance Gilcris	53.67
Paul Cole	118.00
John Croteau	78.83
Bert Lyman	57.17
Wilfred Oakes	58.54
Tom Forbush	52.70
James Croteau	62.04
Sam Pearson	21.00
Clifton Abbott	39.27
Walter Perkins	67.28
Samuel Oakes	28.97
R. C. Montgomery	32.28
J. E. Montgomery	113.00
Len Peabody	59.50
Alex Silver	43.17
Vernon Bickford	135.64
Ernest Kiser, gravel	37.70
Paul Cole, gravel	3.70

$2,126.42

Detail 19. Interest:
  Payment on temporary loans................ $ 972.50
Detail 20. Indebtedness:
  Payment on temporary loans, Coos
    County National Bank.................. $14,000.00

Detail 21. Payments to other governmental
    divisions:
Payment to State, tax.............................$1,134.00
Payment to County, tax........................ 1,888.47
Payments to school district:
Stark School District 4,700.00

                                                    $7,722.47

    Total payments for all purposes........ $48,802.69
    Cash on hand 763.00

    Grand total $49,565.69
                    Respectfully submitted,
                        J. E. MONTGOMERY,
                        E. A. SCOTT,
                        ALBERT EMERY,
                                Selectmen of Stark.
  I have examined the foregoing accounts and find them correct.
                        H. PIKE, *Auditor.*

Road Agents' Report

Town Road, 1931-32
Robert J. Emerson, Road Agent, West End

Royal Montgomery and truck	$ 77.00
Paul St. Frances	139.51
Amos Emery, team and truck	162.75
E. A. Scott, team and truck	143.00
Ernest Kiser and truck	43.50
Harold Pearson	82.25
Eugene Basset	24.50
Dan Cowen	5.25
William Emery	9.92
Norman Hickey	36.75
Frank Gipson	8.75
Henry Gipson	3.50
Bert Emery	81.08
Riley Lunn	35.50
H. W. Stone	1.17
Archie Schoff	14.00
Albert Jackson Estate, gravel	7.40
Frank Smith Corp., rendrock and tools	28.20
Paul Cole, man, team and truck	17.45
Paul Cole, gravel	2.60
Arthur Hamel	54.25
George Hamel	8.75
Eddie Hamel	28.00
Gilbert Hickey	38.50
Eddie Tilton	10.50
Barzel Emery	28.00
Lewis Parker	35.00
Oliver Wood	3.50
S. R. Veazey	31.50
On Holbrook, for gravel	2.00
Albert Scott	10.50
Glenn Lunn	3.50
Groveton Heating & Plumbing Co., tools	2.50
George Goodwin, hardwood plank	2.50
Guy Stone, horses	10.50

A. A. Potter and team	27.12
Hugh Cole and team	4.67
C. E. Buzzell, culverts	17.40
C. W. Potter	3.50
Hazen Cole, sharpening tools	1.50
R. J. Emerson and truck	566.75
R. J. Emerson, gravel	2.43
C. E. Buzzell, culvert	17.40

$1,834.35

ROBERT J. EMERSON.

Ernest Kiser, Road Agent, East End of Town

Ernest Kiser and truck	$ 898.02
Albert Lapointe	121.25
Samuel Oakes	122.00
Wilfred Oakes	101.25
Alix Silver	17.50
George Hill	92.75
Frank Hall	56.00
Harold Pearson	6.00
Orion Leighton	10.60
Gilbert Hickey	7.00
Ethel Miles and team	49.00
Hugh Cole and team	24.50
John Pepaw	10.50
Elworth Scott and team	18.00
Amos Emery and team	7.99
Albert Emery and team	61.00
Elmer McFarland	10.50
Grand Trunk Railroad	21.68
Perry Abbott, sharpening drills	2.00
C. E. Buzzell, culverts	105.75
Frank Blake, gravel screen	15.00
Orion Leighton, gravel	12.60
Frank Smith & Co., dynamite	5.60
O. E. Jackson, gravel	10.00
George Hill, gravel	1.30
Brown Company, gravel	10.50
Groveton Paper Company, sharpening drills	4.00
Groveton Heating & Plumbing Co., tools	8.00

$1,809.30

ERNEST J. KISER.

Town Treasurer's Report

Receipts
Cash on hand at beginning of year	$ 549.98
Received from Town of Stark	33,606.49
Received from M. A. Osgood, collector	14,275.22
Total receipts	$ 48,431.69

Payments
Town orders	$ 47,668.69
Cash on hand January 31, 1932	763.00
Grand total	$ 48,431.69

Respectfully submitted,
URANIA H. CROTEAU, *Treasurer.*

I have examined the foregoing accounts and find them correct.

H. PIKE, *Auditor.*

Report of School Committee

Comparative Table Showing Receipts and Expenditures for Three Years

	Cost in 1930-31	Probable cost in 1931-32	Estm'd cost in 1932-33
Teachers' salaries	$4,350.00	$4,300.00	$4,400.00
Text books	84.94	85.00	85.00
Scholars' supplies	92.60	85.00	85.00
Flags	10.29	10.00	10.00
Other expenses of instruction	10.00	10.00	10.00
Janitors' salaries	180.00	180.00	180.00
Fuel	122.50	220.00	220.00
Janitors' supplies	10.00	10.00	10.00
Repairs	184.24	150.00	150.00
Medical inspection	25.00	20.00	20.00
Transportation	117.00	108.00	108.00
High school tuition	581.37	600.00	600.00
Salaries of officers	130.00	130.00	130.00
Truant officers and census	20.00	20.00	20.00
Superintendent's salary	257.11	257.11	257.11
Per capita tax	154.00	168.00	168.00
Alteration of building	35.25	35.00	35.00
New equipment	225.00		
Expenses of administration	13.00	10.00	10.00
Total cost	$6,602.30	$6,398.11	$6,498.11

RESOURCES

Cash on hand at beginning of year	$ 326.30	$ 115.39	$ 413.80
State aid	1,522.79	2,021.52	1,971.52
Dog tax	68.60	75.00	75.00
Total (not raised by taxation)	$1,917.69	$2,211.91	$2,460.32
Raised by taxation	4,800.00	4,600.00	
Required to balance budget			$4,037.79
Total resources	$6,717.69	$6,811.91	$6,498.11
Balance at end of year	$ 115.39	$ 413.80	

We recommend an appropriation of $4,200.00 to cover the items outlined above.

Respectfully submitted,
GILBERT ROGERS,
META MONTGOMERY,
UNA COLE,
School Board of Stark.

Financial Report of School District

RECEIPTS
Received from Town	$ 4,868.60
Received from State	1,522.79
Balance July 1, 1930	326.30
	$ 6,717.69

PAYMENTS
School orders	$ 6,602.34
Balance June 30, 1931	115.35
	$ 6,717.69

Respectfully submitted,
URANIA H. CROTEAU,
Treasurer.

I have examined the foregoing accounts and find them correct.

H. PIKE, *Auditor.*

REPORT OF TRUST FUNDS OF THE TOWN OF STARK, N. H., ON JANUARY 31, 1932

Date of Creation	Trust Funds Purpose of Creation	HOW INVESTED	Amount of principal	Rate of Interest	Balance of Income at Beginning of year	Income During Year	Expended During Year	Balance of Income at end of year
Mar. 19, 1919	Katherine Holmes Cemetery Fund, donated by Katherine Holmes	City Savings Bank, Berlin, N. H.	$200.00	4%	$120.07	$12.80	$13.76	$119.11
Mar. 12, 1921	Charles Emery Cemetery Fund, donated by Charles Emery	City Savings Bank, Berlin, N. H.	46.13	4%	20.74	3.47		24.21
	Dexter Cole Cemetery Fund, donated by Dexter Cole	City Savings Bank, Berlin, N. H.	50.00	4%	40.20	3.61		43.87
Nov. 1, 1924	Susanah Jackson Cemetery Fund, donated by Susanah Jackson	Stock in Clyde River Power Co.	200.00					
Oct. 31, 1931	George M. Smith, Cemetery Fund	Gorham Savings Bank, Gorham, N. H.	100.00	4				8.24

This is to certify that the information contained in this report is true and correct, to the best of our knowledge and belief.

E. S. COLE,
J. E. MONTGOMERY, } Trustees

January 31, 1932.

Vital Statistics

BIRTHS REGISTERED IN THE TOWN OF STARK, N. H., FOR THE YEAR ENDING DECEMBER 31, 1931

Date of Birth	Name of Child (if any)	Sex	Living or Stillborn	No. of Child	Color	Name of Father	Maiden Name of Mother	Color of Each	Residence of Parents	Occupation of Father	Birthplace of Father	Birthplace of Mother
Feb. 9	Zanita Helen Pepeau	f	Living	2		John Pepeau	Ethelyn Emery	White	Percy, N.H.	Laborer	Belvidere, Vt.	Stark, N. H.
April 29	Bickford	f	Living	2		Vernon W. Bickford	Beatrice Weagle		Crystal, NH	Laborer	Stark, N. H.	Nova Scotia
May 15	Infant Gilcris	m	Still'brn	2		Albert Gilcris	Emma Merrill		Stark, N.H.	Farmer	Westmore, Vt.	Stark, N. H.
June 20	Infant Rogers	f	Living	5		Theodore Rogers	Mad Ivy		Percy, N.H.	Sion Man.	Sta, N. H.	No, Me.
July 4	Marion E. Merrill	f	Living	3		Fred Merrill	Ruth Miles		Stark, N.H.	Farmer	1 1 ng, Vt.	Albany, Vt.
Oct. 7	George Neil	m	Living	3	White	Neil McKinnon	Eula Leighton		Crystal, NH	Foreman	Sydney, N. S.	Stark, N. H.

MARRIAGES REGISTERED IN THE TOWN OF STARK, N. H., FOR THE YEAR ENDING DECEMBER 31, 1931

Date of Marriage	Place of Marriage	Name and Surname of Groom and Bride	Residence of each at time of marriage	Age of each	Color of each	Occupation of Groom and Bride	Place of Birth of each	Name of Parents	Birthplace of Parents	Occupation	Name, Residence and Official Station of Person by whom married
Aug. 26	Groveton	Arthur Hamel	Marland, N.H.	18	White	Laborer	Berlin, N. H.	Gan Hamel Cicile Gosselin	Quebec Berlin, N. H.	Farmer Housewife	Jas F. Happney Catholic Priest
		Eva Fountaine	Stark, N. H.	17		Millman	Groveton, N. H	Mry Fountaine	Vermont		
Sept. 6	Stratford	John Magoon	Lancaster, N.H.	32		Salesman	Goslin, N. H.	Ele L. H.	Quebec Plainfield, N.H.	Farmer Merchant	Edward M. Fuller Baptist Pastor
		Albertina Jackson	Stark, N. H.	28		Stenographer	Stark, N. H.	Gertrude Kirk Lyman A. Jackson Ala Getchel	Grafton, N. H. Stark, N. H.		
Dec. 26	S.Paris, Me.	Ashley W. Leighton	Stark, N. H.	34		Laborer	Stark, N. H.	John Leighton Lettie Jackson	Dummer, N. H. Stark, N. H.	Farmer Housewife	E. B. Letley Baptist Pastor
		Alice Bennett	S. Paris, Me.	21		Shoeworker	Yarmth, Me.	Daniel F. Bennett Henritta Johnson	Illinois Yarmouth, Me.	Shop Worker Housewife	

DEATHS REGISTERED IN TOWN OF STARK, N. H., FOR THE YEAR ENDING DECEMBER 31, 1931.

Date of Death	Name and Surname of Deceased	Age Years / Months / Days	Place of Death	Sex	Color	Single, married or widowed	Occupation	Birthplace of Father	Birthplace of Mother	Name of Father	Maiden Name of Mother
Feb. 28	Jerie Lary Cole	60 / 6 / 23	Stark, N. H.	m			Housewife	Milan, N. H.	Milan, N. H.	Thomas J. Lary	Sarah Keith
Apr. 2	Albert H. Jackson	71 / 4 / 17	Stark, N. H.	m		w	Farmer	Stark, N. H.	Stark, N. H.	Hiram Jackson	Lu... Rit...
Apr. 29	Clau... Cle...	84 / 10 / 20	Stark, N. H.	f		w		Pittsburgh, N.H.	Chibrook, N. H.	Samuel Day	Cu...
May 15	Infant Gileris	/ /	Stark, N. H.	w				e, Vt.	Stark, N. H.	Gileris	Emira Merrill
May 20	Andrew M... S. Page	93 / /	Stewarts own	m			Retired			Luke Page	Abbegail Dudley
June 20	Infant Rogers	82 / 10 / 18	Plymouth, N.H.	m	All		Retired	Bangor, Me.	Bangor, Me.	Theodore Rogers	Winifred Fluery
Aug. 14	John Ca...	/ /	Percy, N. H.	m	White		Laborer	Stark, N. H.	Canton, Me.	James Croteau	Arlene Lertre...
Sept. 9	Elizabeth Pal...	26 / 4 / 20	Stark, N. H.	f		w	None	Canada	Canada		Nancy Ci...
Oct. 5	Frank C. Stone	87 / 5 / 22	P... ene, R.I.	m		w	Dan... Nurse	Waterford, Vt.	Pa...	Howard Brawn	Dail Holton
Nov. 8	Al... B. Merrill	47 / 4 / 25	Stark, N. H.	f		m				Ca...	
Dec. 4	Charles A. Col...	75 / 5 / 28	Lancaster, N.H.	m		w	Farmer	Stark, N. H.	Stark, N. H.	Col...	Harriet R...

I hereby certify that the above returns are correct, according to the best of my knowledge and belief. STELLA A. LUNN, Town Clerk.

Lightning Source UK Ltd.
Milton Keynes UK
UKHW020632060119
334855UK00006B/190/P